DUBROVNIK

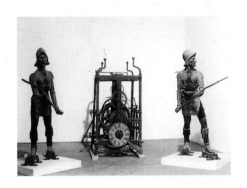

EDITION
SMALL TOURIST MONOGRAPHS

Number 1

ISBN 953-6570-62-9

Editorship
Ana Ivelja-Dalmatin
Mato Njavro
Marija Vranješ
Jasna Vukšić

Text
Ana Ivelja-Dalmatin

Translated from Croatian by
Živan Filippi

Photos
Krešimir Strnad
Turistička naklada archives

Main Editor
Mato Njavro

Publisher
TN *Turistička naklada d.o.o., Zagreb*
Turistički informativni centar, Dubrovnik

For editors
Marija Vranješ
Nino Bagarić

© **COPYRIGHT BY** *Turistička naklada d.o.o., Zagreb*

Preparation of text and photolitographs
Denona d.o.o., Zagreb

Print
Vjesnik d.d., Zagreb

ZAGREB 2001.

"Dubrovnik is not only a work of art but is a creator itself through the centuries. Exposed to influence but always its own. Turned to winds but always steady and firm."

(Jure Kaštelan)

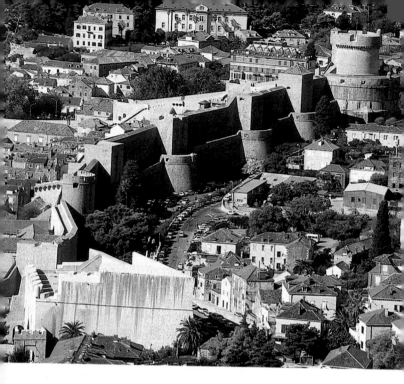

The centuries have left their mark on the stone of city walls, bastions, towers and forts which were the guardians of the cultural heritage of Dubrovnik, defenders of the Citys liberty, and pride, and those of its inhabitants. An unique medieval fortification system, preserved until our day; the work of skilful local and foreign builders. The City is completely encircled by the walls which are the most beautiful and the strongest hymn to freedom.

THE TOWN PROTECTED
BY SVETI VLAHO

"If there were more Dubrovniks in the world, only one of them would be the right one: this true, authentic only Dubrovnik of stones and light. This open palm under stars, extended to the world."

(Jure Kaštelan)

At the very south of the Eastern Adriatic coast, there stands the City – squeezed between sea and mountains, encircled by stone walls, a perfect work of beauty, harmony and nobleness. Nothing will disappoint you in this City; you will absorb its luxury, pass through its streets, and the City itself examines how much you love it, how much you admire it, because here *"... you become enraptured with the rough force of the place conquered by the sea and by stones subjugated by the progressive work of the people in order to serve sensual groves. And all those places where Srd extends its long muscles shine with vines. Confronting winter frosts, Srd defends the inhabitants against the north wind."*

THE DUBROVNIK CLIMATE

"Dubrovnik is a city-chest box, a spiral cradle and a sarcophagus with the nails of the earth and sea, sun and air..."

Dubrovnik is the cultural, historic, maritime and economic centre (49 728 inhabitants), that was included in the UNESCO List of World Natural and Cultural Heritage in 1979. This is a Mediterranean city with plenty of plants brought from all over the world. It lies in the south, among the scent of laurel and rosemary, in the beauty of cypresses and pine. This warm ambience has more than 250 sunny days in the year with a mean annual temperature of 17° C, while a mean summer temperature is 26° C. Snow and low temperatures are very rare, because there is much sunshine here even in winter. January is the coldest month but warmer than in Athens, Cannes or Barcelona, while August is the hottest month and fresher than in Athens. The swimming season lasts from April to October, and there are only 14 rainy days during summer.

The city is protected against the north wind (bura) by Mount Srđ, and against the blows of the south wind (jugo) by the islet of Lokrum. In a gentle Mediterranean landscape, from Neum to the east to Punta Oštro to the west, Dubrovnik stretches with its exciting islands, the romantic Rijeka dubrovačka, the attractive Dubrovnik littoral, the flowery Župa dubrovačka and the fertile Konavle.

IN HISTORIC DURATION

"In front of my eyes, golden centuries of Dubrovnik followed in a row like a necklace."

The centuries have passed and left us this City as inheritance, while it lasts patiently, proud of ascents, gloomy because of declines, but always upright. Dubrovnik has firmly grown into its soil and has woven the roots of an immemorial existence into the present time.

The most recent archeological investigations show that there was an Illyrian settlement on the site of today's Dubrovnik even in the eneolithic period which lived its full spiritual life during the late Hellenic age. Ancient Ragusa was founded on the islet of Laus in the 7th century A.D. Since then, all through the medieval commune until the free Dubrovnik Republic, this southernmost Croatian town has formed its identity and built in its urban network the dream about the beauty for which one lived and died. The first written document about the name Dubrovnik originates from 1189, while the *Statute Liber Statorum Civitatis Ragusii* from 1272 consists of laws and regulations about the internal and foreign political life, administration, maritime trade, building... The history of this City is very long, demonstrating how it managed to preserve its liberty and independence by means of its diplomacy and its courage during numerous centuries. Dubrovnik recognized the supreme power of Byzantium, the Normans, and endured the fifteen-month siege of the Saracens in 866 and 867, while it was under Venetian rule from 1205 to 1358. After liberating itself from the rule of the "Venetian Lion" it recognized formally the sovereignty of the Croato-Hungarian state and developed as an *independent Dubrovnik Republic – Respublica Ragusina.*

This small but wise Republic withstood all attacks, enriched itself, developed, and halted by its skilful diplomacy and strong walls, all those who wanted to plunder and destroy. It even managed to save its autonomy and freedom of trade from the mighty Ottoman Empire before which many stronger states trembled. It did so by paying an annual tribute of 12 500 ducats.

In the 15th and 16th centuries Dubrovnik was at the peak of its development. It encompassed territory from the peninsula of Pelješac to the east to Konavle to the south. The Town was encircled by high walls; planned dwelling building took place with a regular scheme of streets; palaces, churches and monasteries were built. *The Golden Age of Dubrovnik* was the peak of its cultural and economic development with maritime affairs as the most important economic sector, together with the production and export of salt.

The merchant fleet of the Dubrovnik Republic, which consisted of 4000 seamen and more than 180 large ships, was numbered as the strongest in the Mediterranean in the 16th century. Its ships navigated across all the seas and oceans of the world, and the City-state established relationships with the most prominent European centres.

All private interests were subordinated to the benefit of the state. Dubrovnik, during its thousand-year history, never made an aggressive war, but maintained freedom and peace by skilful and wise diplomacy. The Dubrovnik Republic was the first state to recognize the independence of the United States of America.

Peace and prosperity enabled Dubrovnik not only to develop trade, shipbuilding and shipping but also the flourishing of sciences, literature, art, building crafts, goldsmith's trade...

Ingenious and creative minds worked in Dubrovnik or were born there – Marin Držić, Ivan Gundulić, Ruđer Bošković, Marin Getaldić, Nikola Božidarević, Miho Hamzić...

Dubrovnik, as an urban centre, introduced medical care in 1301; opened the first pharmacy in 1317; one of the oldest in Europe which has worked continually up to the present time; established a hospital Domus Christii in 1347; founded a quarantine, the first in the world, in 1377; built a home for foundlings in 1434; and constructed an aqueduct in 1436.

The City was governed by noblemen, the richest class who had all the political power in the state. At the head of the Dubrovnik Republic there were three councils and a rector, elected for a month. The Great Council had legislative power, the Small Council had executive power, while the real power was in the Senate.

In 1667 a severe earthquake all but destroyed the city. A great part of the city was destroyed, many valuables were lost in fire, and many citizens were killed. The City recovered slowly but it did not give up.

The beginning of the 19th century meant for Dubrovnik the last days of its centuries-long autonomy. Napoleon's marshal Marmont abolished

7

the free Dubrovnik Republic on January 31, 1808.

Dubrovnik continued to live through stormy days under the rule of Austria, France, England, Russia and Turkey. Times were hard also during the old Yugoslavia and the fascist occupation in the Second World War. However, the City in which *"freedom cannot be sold for all the gold of the world"*, endured in 1991 and 1992 maybe the greatest aggression in its thousand-year old history – the Serbian and Montenegrin killing of its people and shelling of its buildings. Courageous and defiant, Dubrovnik proved that only *"freedom is the measure of freedom"* and it returned hatred with goodness, beauty and truth.

Dubrovnik is not limited by time, it is timeless, always different, a unique City.

THE CITY-MONUMENT

"Dubrovnik is the city of an almost perfect human measure."

For some people Dubrovnik is the city of art, for some others the city of noble architecture, for some the city of history, a city adorned by poets and painters, but Dubrovnik is all that together. This city-monument has sublimated in itself both culture and art, history and contemporaneity. Stone is the ruler in this City, the stone of its streets, squares, palaces, houses and churches, quiet and vivacious, perfect and stable, of an immortal beauty. History and man were building this city by patiently incorporating in it all silver, all gold, all human lives.

In the oldest parts of ancient *Ragusa*, called *Pustijerna, Karmen and Sveta Marija*, narrow stone streets, shady "volti", old palaces guarded the spirit of the city, while medieval walls, built and rebuilt in the hardest times from the 13th to the 17th centuries, were its defence and protection. *The walls* are 1940 metres long, are 4-6 metres thick towards the land, and 1,3-3 towards the sea, and they were at some places up to 25 metres high. This fortification system is today the system of beauty, a designation which gives it a unique and recognizable appearance. Four outstanding points of the city are protected by fortifications. To the north, there is the monumental round *Minčeta*, completed in 1464, built by numerous builders, among them the famous Juraj Dalmatinac; to the east, the mighty *Revelin*, built in 1462 against the Turkish danger; to the southeast, the imposing fort *Sveti Ivan* from the 16th century, the work of the Dubrovnik builder Paskoje Miličević, protected the entrance to the old city port, and to the west, the entrance to the city is defended by the harmonious *Bokar* (Star-lit), which was built by the Florentine Michelozzo from 1461 to 1463. The mighty and autonomous Fort *Lovrijenac* defends the town to the west against the danger both from sea and land. It was built on the rock 37 metres high and it originates, according to legend, from the 11th century, while reliable data puts it in the 14th century. Together with these strongest fortifications, the walls consist of two more round towers, 12 square ones, 5 bastions and two angle towers. The walls towards the land had an additional deep moat, while in the time of greatest danger the city was defended by 120 cannons worked in local workshops. The best known cannon smelter in the 16th century was Ivan Rabljanin. *The City Port*, to which all the riches of Dubrovnik used to arrive, was protected from waves and sudden attacks by the break-water Kaše. One could enter it through two gates, *Vrata od Ponte* (port) and *Vrata od Ribarnice*.

Two fortified city gates gave entrance to the City: the east *Vrata od Ploča* from the 15th century and the west *Vrata od Pila* from 1537. During the time of the Republic, the draw bridge of Vrata od Pila was raised by strong chains and closed the entrance to the City. The stone figure of sv. Vlaho watches over this gate

through which one enters the old city centre and its main street *Plaza*, the famous *Stradun*, a unique and unforgettable place with the fine stone facades of dwelling houses. The Stradun is the most beautiful and largest city street which connects the west and east entrances to the City. This unique space is the favourite promenade, the place of meeting and talk, processions and festivities and also the main merchant street. Two fountains close it – *Velika Onofrijeva fontana* (Large Onofri'o Fountain), built by the Neapolitan builder Onofrio della Cava, with its 16 masques from which water flows, and another *Mala fontana* (Small Fountain) under the City Bell-tower, the work of Petar Martinov from Milan. Opposite Velika fontana there is the small votive *church of sv. Spas* from 1520, which remained undamaged in the great earthquake from 1667. This Renaissance small church is the work of the Korčula master Petar Andrijić. The monumental complex of *Franjevački samostan male braće* (the Franciscan Monastery of Small Brothers) from the 14th century continues and extends to Minčeta, while the side facade of the church looks towards the Stradun, with its door arched with the luxurious Gothic portal, the only one preserved in the earthquake. It is the work of Korčula masters brothers Andrijić from 1498, while the central stone *Pieta* testifies to the beauty and splendour of this monastery. But the most beautiful part of this space is the High Romanesque cloister from 1360, the building masterpiece of Mihoje Brajkov from Bar. Harmonious double hexaphores have each a different luxurious capital. *The pharmacy*, the third oldest in Europe, has continuously been in use here since 1317. A rich library has also been preserved with 20 000 books, of which especially valuable are old manuscripts (1 200 copies) and 137 incunabula. The museum collection exhibits valuable works of art, the original inventory of the old pharmacy, the paintings of old masters, and objects of the goldsmith's craft.

Not far away from Franjevački samostan and Velika Onofrijeva fontana, next to the city walls, there was the convent, *Samostan sv. Klare*, built in the 13th and 14 centuries, where there was a home for foundlings in 1434.

At the east part of the Stradun, there extends *Trg Luža* (Luža Square), a picturesque ambience in whose middle there is the famous *Orlandov stup* (Orlando's Column), built by the master Antun Dubrovčanin, while the most significant administrative and church buildings are around it.

Each year on July 10, the opening of Dubrovački ljetni festival (the Dubrovnik Summer Festival) takes place, while the festival flag is hoisted to Orlando's Column, waving until the closing of this unique manifestation on August 25.

During this Festival, ever since that distant year 1950, the whole city has been transformed into theatre, while its picturesque streets become unique stages under the open sky for theatre and music performances.

The medieval warrior Orlando, with his shield and sword, backs on to the Baroque *church of sv. Vlaho* (Saint Blaise), the patron of the city of Dubrovnik since the 10th century. The church was built between 1706 and 1715 by the Venetian builder Marino Gropelli. It was built on the site of the previous old Romanesque church, which survived the great earthquake of 1667, but which was completely destroyed in the fire of 1706. The interior of the church is richly decorated, while the statue of sv. Vlaho of silver gilt is on the main altar. This is the work of the Dubrovnik school of art from the 15th century. Sv. Vlaho keeps in his hand the scale model of the Dubrovnik before the earthquake. This statue survived fire by some miracle. February 3, the day of the patron of

The small church of sv. Marija (15th c.) on Danče hosts the most beautiful works of the Dubrovnik School of Painting. The triptych Our Lady With Saints from 1517 is the last work of the master Nikola Božidarević.

Dubrovnik, is celebrated solemnly every year.

Opposite the church of sv. Vlaho, there is *Palača Sponza* (the Sponza Palace), the most beautiful Dubrovnik palace, built from 1516 onwards by local masters, Paskoje Miličević and brothers Andrijić. During the time of the Republic, the custom-office, the state mint, the bank, the state treasury, and the armory were there. This sumptuous Gothic-Renaissance palace survived the earthquake and testified to the richness of the City; it was the meeting place of merchants and businessmen, while Dubrovnik poets from the 16th century founded in it the Academy of the Unanimous, the first literary institution in Dubrovnik. Today, this palace hosts the "very republic of papers" – *the archives of Dubrovnik* with rich archival material and precious historic documents.

Next to Sponza there is *Luža zvonara* (Luža of Bell-ringers), which summoned the Council by its bells, called the alarm and other dangers. Next to it there is *Gradski zvonik sa satom* (the Clock Tower), built in 1444, it is 31 metres high with huge bells cast in 1509 by Ivan Rabljanin, on which the bronze figures "green ones" strike the hours. The building of Gradska straža (the City Guard), from 1490, was important for the security of the Republic with a flat for the admiral. Then the Gothic-Renaissance palace of Veliko vijeće (the Big Council Palace) continues and links itself with *Knežev dvor* (the Rector's Palace), a representative monument of secular architecture which was the centre of power and administration for the Dubrovnik Republic.

This beautiful Gothic-Renaissance palace was being built and rebuilt for centuries, and was damaged by fires, explosions of gunpowder and earth-quakes. As well as the Rector's cabinet and his private rooms, there was here the seat of the Small Council and of the Republic administration, a hall for receptions, and also the armory, the gunpowder store and the prison. Today, the Rector's Palace is an unique museum which has preserved its stylish furniture, portraits and coat-of-arms of Dubrovnik nobility, the paintings of old masters, a numismatic collection of the coins during the Dubrovnik Republic, the original keys of the city gate and many other valuables. The Senate decided in 1638 to put, in the atrium of the Rector's Palace, a bronze bust of the rich seaman from Lopud, Miho Pracat. He was a meritorious citizen and the only plebeian to whom the Republic erected a monument. The arched doorway is ornamented with luxuriously chiselled, capitals.

Fort Lovrijenac built on the 37-metre high rock, is one of the pillars of the defense of Dubrovnik, both against attacks from the sea and from the land. This dominant fort watches over possible enemy attacks and has walls up to 12 metres thick, while the part turned towards the city walls is only 60 cm thick. Wise men of Dubrovnik were cautious not only towards outside enemies but also towards the possible taking over of the Fort's command power.

Mighty Minčeta with its magnificent battlements is the most glorious tower of Dubrovnik built in the 14th and 15th centuries with an unforgettable view to the City. It dominates the City with its height and monumentality and it is also the highest point of Dubrovnik's walls. It was built by famous local and foreign builders, among them the Renaissance master Juraj Dalmatinac who continued to work on the fort after the Florentine Michelozzo.

The Pile Gate is the west entrance to the City built from the 14th to the 16th centuries.

Near the Rector's Palace, in a large square, the Dubrovnik *cathedral of Uznezenja Marijina* (Our Lady's Assumption) was erected in the 13th century. According to legend, the Romanesque cathedral which was destroyed in the earthquake of 1667, had been built by the money of King Richard the Lion Heart who survived a shipwreck near Lokrum returning from the Third Crusade in 1192. Investigations have shown that even before the Romanesque cathedral was destroyed in the earthquake there existed a cathedral from the 7th century. The amazing Riznica katedrale (the Treasury of the Cathedral) with priceless artistic riches has been preserved under the turquoise dome which dominates the City. The golden reliquaries of St. Blaise's head and legs from the 11th and 12th centuries, silver reliquaries, crosses and church plates, as well as the paintings of old masters, are especially valuable.

To the west of the Cathedral, there is *Gundulićeva poljana* (the Gundulić marketplace), a spacious square which transforms itself during the day to a colourful and vivacious marketplace and which is dominated by the bronze monument to the poet of liberty, Ivan Gundulić.

The most beautiful Baroque stairway *Uz Jezuite* (Past the Jesuits) from 1738 begins from the Gundulić marketplace and leads to a large area named by the great astronomer and philosopher, Poljana Ruđera Boškovića. Here is the Jesuit *church of sv. Ignacije* (17th – 18th c.), illustrated with Baroque frescos with the scenes from St. Ignatius's life.

Not far away is *Žitnica Rupe* (the Rupe Granary), built in the 16th century with 15 big dry cisterns with a capacity of 150 wagons of wheat grain. The Dubrovnik republic took care to have enough wheat in case of bad years or a siege.

Dominikanski samostan (the Dominican Monastery) protected by the strong Revelin is situated on the east part of the town. This is an outstanding architectural complex and the richest treasury of cultural and artistic heritage in Dubrovnik. The monastery was built in the 14th century with a large church whose south Gothic portal is the work of the sculptor Bonino da Milano from 1419. The Gothic-Renaissance cloister whose arches are closed by triphoras with fine rosettes is of outstanding beauty. There is a luxurious stone well in the courtyard of the cloister. The monastery museum exhibits priceless riches. Besides valuable manuscripts and incunabula, gold and silver jewellery by famous Dubrovnik goldsmiths, the most valuable being the collection of the creation of *Dubro-*

The Dubrovnik Stradun – Plaza is the most famous Dubrovnik street, a favourite promenade and meeting place which received its today's appearance after the great earthquake in 1667.

vačka slikarska škola (the Dubrovnik School of Painting) from the 15th and 16th centuries with the works of Lovro Dobričević, Mihajlo Hamzić and Nikola Božidarević; also the large painted crucifixion by Paolo Venezin from the 14th century, the altar painting of St. Magdalene, a Titian's work from 1550.

From the Dominican Monastery, we can pass through a shady street and come to *Prijeko*, a picturesque street parallel with the Stradun on whose east end is *Crkvica sv. Nikole* (St. Nicholas's church) from the 11th century, one of the oldest preserved Dubrovnik churches.

On *Ploče*, the east part of the city outside the city walls, next to the sea there are lazarets, built from the 16th to the 18th centuries, where quarantine was arranged in order to prevent contagious diseases and epidemics possibly transmitted by seamen and merchants.

There is a nice view from Ploče to *Lokrum*, an islet covered with dense green woods which surround a previous Benedictine monastery from the 12th century. This is a romantic islet of gentle coves, shady promenades, dense subtropical plants and an unique Mrtvo more (the Dead Sea), a salty small lake connected with the sea. *Pile* is a western part of the City which has always been a traffic and tourist cross-roads. At the foot of Fort Lovrijenac, there is the oldest small Dubrovnik port, Kolorina, and the *park Gradac* is nearby with a magnificent view to the City and the sea. A path towards the sea leads from the park to *Danče*, which are mentioned in documents as "lazareti", the last shelter for those sick of plague. *Crkvica sv. Marije* (the small St. Mary's Church) hosts the most beautiful paintings of the Dubrovnik school of painting – a polyptych by Lovro Dobričević and a triptych by Nikola Božidarević.

West from the old city centre in a secluded bay, there is *Gruž*, old Gravosia, the centre of today's maritime and bus traffic. Touching Gruž, the wooded peninsula *Lapad* continues with its attractive family houses, comfortable hotels and tourist facilities.

"Those who look for a paradise on earth should come and see Dubrovnik."

(Bernard Shaw)

The votive Renaissance church of sv. Spas from 1520, which survived the disastrous earthquake, is the work of the Korčula master Petar Andrijić.

The large Onofrio Fountain was built in 1438 by the Neapolitan master Onofrio della Cava who brought water to the City from the source in Rijeka Dubrovačka.

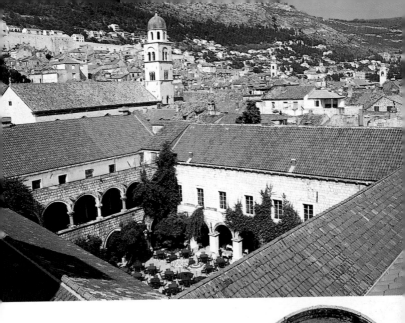

Next to the city walls, Sv. Klara's convent was
built in the 13th and 14th centuries which
founded also a home for foundlings in 1434.

Sv. Vlaho was venerated as the patron
of Dubrovnik even in the 10th century.
The men of Dubrovnik built churches
to their patron, placed his statues, his
figure was on the state flag and stamp
as well as on coins.

The south part of the mighty Dubrovnik walls was built on steep cliffs which descend to the sea. Fort Bokar, built in the 15th century to defend the Pile Gate, is of an exceptional beauty.

Dubrovnik

The luxurious interior of the Franciscan church from the 17th c

The portal of the Franciscan church from the 15th century was made by the brothers Leonardo and Petar Petrović in their stone-mason's workshop.

Within the walls of the Franciscan Monastery there is the old pharmacy from 1317 which has continually served up to the present day and is one of the oldest in Europe.

Dubrovnik

The Romanesque cloister of the Franciscan Monastery from 1360 is a harmonious space made by Mihoje Brajkov from Bar.

Lovro Dobričević, created the Figure of sv. Vlaho, in the 15th c., the Franciscan Monastery.

The garden and the fountain of the Franciscan Monastery, the 15th c.

Dubrovnik

Picturesque old Dubrovnik roofs and the green islet of Lokrum.

One of the narrow steep Dubrovnik streets with numerous steps.

The interior of the Dubrovnik synagogue, one of the oldest in Europe, whose beginnings go back to the 14th century.

The Small Fountain, erected in 1438 according to the plan by Onofrio della Cava; it is decorated by the sculptor Petar Martinov from Milan.

The interior of the Dominican church from the 15th century.

A richly decorated well in the courtyard of the Dominican Monastery.

The Romanesque portal on the south facade of the Dominican church is the work of Bonino from Milan, 15th century.

The Dominican Monastery, Triptych, the work of Miho Hamzić from 1512.

The Dominican Monastery, the altar painting Sv. Magdalena, Titian's work, the 15th century.

The Dominican Monastery, Annunciation, Nikola Božidarević's work from 1513.

The Dominican Monastery, the altar painting St. Dominic's Miracle, Vlaho Bukovac's work.

The Dominican Monastery, the polyptych Christ's Baptism, Lovro Dobričević's work from 1448.

The Ploče Gate, the east entrance to the city, built in the 15th century. It has both outside and inside gates above which the tower Asimon (Kula od Ploča) rises and protects them.

The old city port from which Dubrovnik sailing ships used to depart to the world's oceans and in which they were built and repaired.

Porporela, praised in song, and the monumental St. John's Fort which protected the entrance to the city port and was one of the most important defense fortifications of the City.

At the place where today's Cathedral of Maria's Assumption stands, built in the 18th century according to the plan of the Italian architect Buffalini from Urbina, there existed two other cathedrals, a Byzantine one from the 7th century and the Romanesque one from the 12th century, a sumptuous stone building which was destroyed in the great earthquake in 1667.

In the luxurious interior of the Dubrovnik Cathedral, especially valuable are Titian's painting Maria's Assumption from the 16th century above the main altar, and the unique altar of Sv. Ivan Nepomuk, built in 1758 from pink marble.

The Cathedral Treasury, Our Lady with the Child (Madonna della Seggiola) is ascribed to Raffael, the 15th century.

In the Cathedral Treasury there is the replica of sv. Vlaho's head from the 11th and 13th centuries in the form of the crown of Byzantine emperors in enamel and precious stones, a valuable work of Dubrovnik goldsmiths.

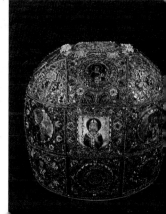

43

The Cathedral Treasury is an amazing space with priceless riches. It exhibits gold and silver reliquaries, crosses, church plates and paintings of Italian, Flemish and local masters.

The Baroque stairway from 1738 Past the Jesuits leads from the Gundulićeva poljana to Boškovićeva poljana where there is the imposing Baroque Jesuit church of sv. Ignacije built in the 17th and 18th centuries next to which Collegium Ragusinum, the famous Dubrovnik college is placed.

Dubrovnik

The unforgettable Dubrovnik Stradun and Orlando's Column.

The bronze statue of the Dubrovnik poet of liberty, Ivan Gundulić, dominates picturesque Gundulićeva poljana; it is the work of Ivan Rendić from 1892. There are four bas-reliefs on the pedestal of the monument with scenes from the epic Osman.

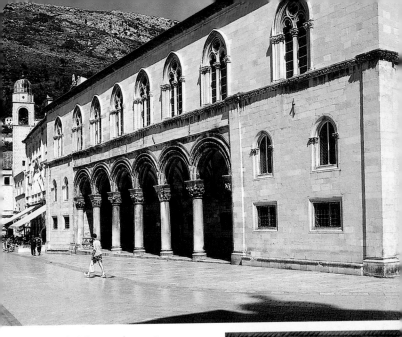

The Rector's Palace is a harmonious Gothic-Renaissance palace from the 15th century, the seat of rule and administration of the Dubrovnik Republic.

According to the decision of the Senate from 1638, Miho Pracat's bust was placed in the atrium of the Rector's Palace; he was a meritorious citizen and donor, a rich shipowner from Lopud, the only plebeian to whom the Dubrovnik Republic erected a monument.

47

The work room of the Dubrovnik Rector in the Rector's Palace.

The big stone column decorated by the figure of the medieval knight Orlando was built in the 15th century by the sculptor Bonino from Milan. The length of the elbow from his right hand was taken as a measure of length, so called the Dubrovnik elbow (51,2 cm).

The magnificent arched doorway of the Rector's Palace with lovely capitals made by the master Petar Martinov from Milan.

The Baroque church of sv. Vlaho, the patron of the city. It was built in 1715 according to the plan of the Venetian builder Marin Groppeli with a richly decorated portal and a large stairway. On February 3 every year, the public/church holiday of sv. Vlaho is celebrated.

Luža Square, a picturesque Dubrovnik area with representative administrative and church buildings, the place where the solemn opening of the Dubrovnik Festival takes place every year.

The grand steps in front of the entrance to sv. Vlaho's church is a pleasant place for rest and a break.

The statue of sv. Vlaho of silver gilt from the 15th century is the work of an unknown Dubrovnik master. The saints holds in his left hand the scale model of the city of Dubrovnik before the great earthquake of 1667.

The Gothic-Renaissance Sponza Palace is one of the most beautiful Dubrovnik palaces built according to the master Paskoje Miličević's plan.

Dubrovnik

The interior courtyard of the Sponza Palace was the meeting-place of merchants and businessmen. The following Latin inscription has been preserved on the atrium arch where the pair of scales hung before: *FALLERE NOSTRA VETANT, ET FALLI PONDERA, MEQVE PONDERO CVM MERCES, PONDERAT IPSE DEVS (Our weights do not allow to cheat and to be cheated. When I measure goods I am measured by God himself.)*

The unique Stradun – Plaza, is the main, largest noisiest and the most favourite Dubrovnik street. The unforgettable encounter with the City begins here where everything happens. It was built after the great earthquake of 1667.

A City of stone, on stone, built for eternity. The City according to the measure of man who prized freedom above everything.

Oh beautiful, dear freedom,
the gift in which all riches were given to us by God,
you are the true cause of all our glory,
the only adornment of this Grove,
all silver, all gold, all human lives
cannot repay your clean beauty.
(Ivan Gundulić)

Dubrovnik is a city one never forgets. Its beauty, harmony and nobility is always remembered.

Prijeko street is a picturesque city ambience transformed into an unique restaurant under the open sky.

Forts Lovrijenac and Minčeta are the most significant defensive points of the City. There is an inscription on Lovrijenac: NON BENE PRO TOTO LIBERTAS VENDITUR AURO (Freedom cannot be sold for all the gold).

Dubrovnik and Lokrum – The City and its island.

The islet of Lokrum within reach of Dubrovnik holds in its green surfaces the previous Benedictine Monastery from the 12th century, as well as the memories of the rulers who enjoyed its beauty.

The cross on Mount Srd is the symbol of endurance, pride and obstinacy of this city and its inhabitants. Dubrovnik is amazing, the city of infinite beauty and splendour which immortalized in itself the gift of nature and human strength.

The Renaissance Petar Sorkočević's castle in Lapad from the 16th century is a luxurious summer residence with beautiful terraces, a lake and gardens. Together with other country buildings, this castle marks a rich life of entertainment and rest lived by noble Dubrovnik families in their summer villas where masked dances, theatre performances and literary evenings took place.

To the west from the old city centre, the woody peninsula of Lapad extends with modern hotels, family villas and rich tourist facilities. The tourist settlement Babin kuk offers numerous tourist challenges amidst the beauty of the sea and sun.

Rijeka dubrovačka – A picturesque stretch of the Ombla river.

Zaton – Veliki and Mali, two picturesque settlements in a sheltered cove.

Trsteno – Arboretum,
a sumptuous botanic
garden from the 16th
century.

Slano – The Osmine hotel
surrounded by dense Medi-
terranean vegetation.

 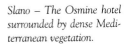

Mali Ston, a small town of harmonious architecture and strong towers and bastions.

Ston, a medieval town with impressive serpentine defense walls from the 14th and 15th centuries and its natural salt-pans rich in "white gold", the precious product of the Dubrovnik Republic.

The oyster breeding site in the Bay of Mali Ston.

69

The island of Koločep or Kalamota is one of the Elaphite Islands of an undisturbed beauty and mild climate with two settlements, Gornje Čelo and Donje Čelo. The island of seamen and sea captains was mentioned for the first time by its present day name in the 14th century although it was inhabited even in Hellenic times. The men of Koločep were well-known as coral divers who engaged themselves in this dangerous occupation even in the 14th century. The small church of sv. Anton Opat holds the valuable painting Our Lady with Saints from 1434 by the painter Ivan Ugrinović.

The island of Lopud is the most economically developed among Elaphite islands. Its only settlement is Lopud, situated in a sheltered cove, from which a one kilometre long path leads to the opposite side of the island and to the Šunj bay with its nice sandy beach. This is the island of valuable monuments, churches, summer residences and tourist facilities. Miho Pracat, a shipowner and benefactor of the Dubrovnik Republic, was born and bred on the island of Lopud.

The island of Mljet, our most wooded island with rich Mediterranean vegetation, clear sea, a stormy history, valuable cultural heritage and colourful folk costumes. The west part of the island was proclaimed a National Park due to its natural characteristics.

According to legend this island was by Odysseus and the nymph tarried on Calypso; the apostle Paul stayed for a while here.

The islet of sv. Marija in the middle of the Big Lake on which the monastery and the church were built in the 12th century, on Mljet.

The island of Šipan, the biggest among the Elaphite Islands and the richest one in monuments. Today's name was mentioned in 1370. During the Dubrovnik Republic it had its own Rector whose seat was in the Rector's Palace in Šipanska Luka. Valuable sacred buildings, monuments and summer residences have been preserved of which the most representative ones are the those in the ownership of Tomo and Vice Stjepović-Skočibuha from the 16th century. Oil and wine from Šipan are well-known all over the world.

Pomena – The Odisej hotel is situated in this attractive Mediterranean landscape, in a gentle and wooded cove.

Mlini, in times past the seat of the miller's craft, is situated in the shady Župski zaljev, the ancient Dubrovnik Astarea, in a gentle landscape, next to the small Zavrelje river which flows into the sea nearby. This place of rest and holiday offers numerous tourist facilities. The past of this region has been preserved in monuments, inscribed in documents, lived through in poems and songs, customs, colourful folk costumes. A church was erected to the honour of sv. Ilar, a hermit and patron saint who annihilated here the dragon of paganism.

The Župa settlements Mlini and Srebreno in which the beauty of nature and the love of man are interwoven.

Plat "in the colours of the sea and light, in the twinkles of the wind and air."

The men of Župa keep proudly their rich folk costumes, "golden robe" embroidered with golden warps.

Glowing fruits of the strawberry tree, or arbutus.

Cavtat, ancient Epidaurum, from whose ruins today's small town arose, is ideally situated on a green peninsula. It recalls the Illyrians, Greek and Romans, destructive invasions of Slavonic and Avarian tribes in the 7th century, and the glorious Dubrovnik Republic. Cavtat is the town of the writer and collector Baltazar Bogišić, the politician Frano Supilo and the famous painter Vlaho Bukovac. It has preserved its valuable historic buildings – the Rector's Palace, the Baroque church of sv. Nikola from the 14th century, the Franciscan Monastery of Our Lady of the Snow – various collections, etc.

Cavtat is a small town of tourist challenges, luxurious hotels, steep shady streets and flowery gardens. The Croatia hotel fits harmoniously into the beauty of the landscape.

The family Račić mausoleum was built in 1922 and is one of the most beautiful mausoleums made by the great sculptor Ivan Meštrović.

Čilipi – Traditional Sunday folklore performances take place in front of the church of sv. Nikola. Visitors will be thrilled with the original dances from Konavle, luxurious folk costumes and rich folk handicrafts.

The airport "Dubrovnik" in Čilipi.

An attractive excursion centre and the restaurant "Konavoski dvori" have been arranged at the source of the Ljuta river with local specialities and quality wines.

Molunat, a picturesque Konavle settlement situated in a sheltered cove covered with exuberant Mediterranean vegetation.

Oranges, golden fruits of the south.

Konavle, a gentle ambience of clear water, tall cypresses and stormy history. Only a "palm of soil" and my native place.

Wedding folk costumes from Konavle enriched by gold embroidery are the reflection of dignity and beauty of this region and its people.

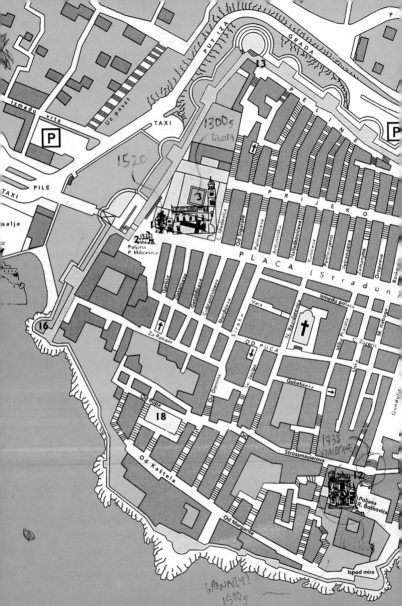

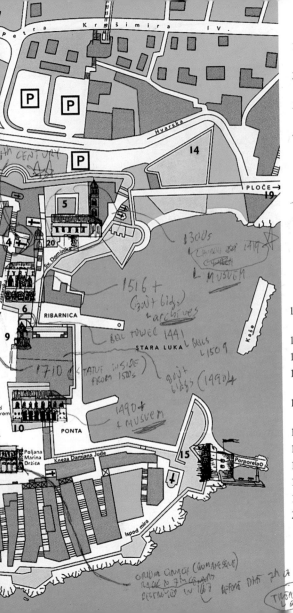

1. The Church of St. Salvation
2. The Large Onofrio Fountain
3. The Franciscan Monastery
4. The Church of St. Nicola
5. The Dominican Monastery
6. The Sponza Palace
7. The Orlando Column
8. St. Blaise's Church
9. The Small Fountain
10. The Rector's Palace
11. The Cathedral
12. The Jesuit Church
13. The Minčeta Tower
14. The Revelin Tower
15. Fort St. John
16. Fort Bokar
17. Fort Lovrijenac
18. Museum Rupe
19. The Art Galery
20. Galery "Sebastian"

Dubrovnik – the Dominican Monastery, Our Lady with Saints,
Nikola Božidarević's work, the 16th century.

"Dubrovnik is the work of love."

Dubrovnik, the church of sv. Marija on Danče, Polyptych,
Lovro Dobričević's work, the 15th century.

TOURIST INFORMATION

Important telephones

Ambulance Station	94
Information Centre	985
Police	92
Information	
(local)	988
(outside)	981, 989
Telegrams	96
Alarm Clock	9101
Exchange Rate	9864
Conditions on Roads	9866
International Calls	901

Travel agencies

Alpe-Adria tours, N. Tesle 2

Atlas,
Branch Office Pile, dr. A. Starčevića 1
Branch Office Gruž, Gruška obala
Branch Office Lapad, V. Lisinskoga 5
Branch Office Ploče, F. Supila 2

Atlantska plovidba
(maritime travel agencz),
Gruž, Obala S. Radića 26
Lapad, N. Tesle 14

DBS, F. Supila 5

Generalturist, F. Supila 9

Globtour, Zeljarica 5/II
Branch Office Stradun, Placa

Madra, I. Vojnovića 69

OK travel & trade, Obala S. Radića 32

REA, Gruška obala 1

**Tourist Information Centre (TIC)
"Stradun"**, Placa 1

Association of Tourist Guides,
Bunićeva poljana

Hotels

"L" category

Dubrovnik-President, Babin kuk

Villa Orsula, Put F. Supila 14

"A" category

Argentina, Put F. Supila 14

Excelsior, Put F. Supila 12

Villa Dubrovnik, V. Bukovca 6

"B" category

Adriatic, Masarykov put 9

Argosy, Babin kuk

Bellevue, P. Čingrije 7

Komodor, Masarykov put 5

Kompas, Put kardinala Stepinca

Lapad, Lapadska obala 37

Lero, I. Vojnovića 14

Mali Imperial, M. Blažića 2

Minčeta, Babin kuk

Neptun, Put kardinala Stepinca

Park, Šetalište kralja Zvonimira 3

Petka, Obala S. Radića 38

Splendid, Masarykov put 8

Sumratin, Šetalište kralja Zvonimira 31

Vis, Masarykov put 4

Omladinski hostel (Youth Hostel),
Bana J. Jelačića 15/17

Restaurants

Adria, Čubranovićeva 4

Amfora, Obala S. Radića 26

Antunini, Prijeko 30

Atlas Club Nautika, Brsalje 3

Domino, Od Domina 6

Dubrovnik, M. Kaboge 5

Eden, Kardinala Stepinca 54

Gorica, M. Kaboge 1

Jadran, Poljana Miličevića 1

Komin, Babin kuk

Konavoka, Šetalište kralja Zvonimira 38

Konoba Dundo Maroje, Kovačka b.b.

Konoba Marko Polo, Lučarica 6

Lapad, Šetalište kralja Zvonimira 3

Maestoso, Kralja Tomislava 1

Minčeta (Robna kuća), N. Tesle 2

Moby Dick, Prijeko 20a

Nada, Žudioska 8

Orhan, Od Tabakarije 1

Orsan, I . Zajca 2

Primorka, N. Tesle 7

Porat, Obala S. Radića 30

Ragusa 2, Zamanjina 12

Rozarij, Zlatarska 4

Sebastian, Prijeko 11

Srđ (Robna kuća), S. Radića 25

Taxi Stations

Autobusni kolodvor, Put Republike

Pile, Brsalje

Gruž, Luka Gruž (ispred Jadrolinije)

Ploče, F. Supila

Rent-a-car

Budget, Obala S. Radića 20

Dubrovnik, Obala S. Radića 29

No 5, Ispod Petke 5

Zadarkomerc, I. Vojnovića 57

Museums

Aquarium (Fort sv. John), D. Jude 12

Dubrovnik museum,
Rector's Palace, Pred Dvorom 3

Marin Držić House , Široka ulica 1

City Walls, Sv. Dominika 3

Ethnographic Museum Rupe, Od Rupa

Dominican Monastery Museum,
Sv. Dominika 4

**Franciscan Monastery Museum
"Mala braća"**, Placa 2

Monastery Sigurate Museum,
Od Sigurate 13

Maritime Museum (Fort St. John)

Cathedral Treasury,
  Kneza Damjana Jude 1
Synagogue, Židoska 5

Galleries

Art Gallery, Put. F. Supila 23

Sebastian, Sv. Dominika 5

Sebastian Stradun, Placa

Ars Longa – Vita Brevis, Pred Dvorom

Art Gallery "Studio", Prijeko 21 a

"Placa" Gallery, Placa

"Lacroma" Gallery,
  Kneza Damjana Jude 6

"Sv. Luka" Gallery,
  Između Vrata od Ploča b.b.

"Otok" Club Gallery, Pobijana 8

"Klarisa" Gallery,
  Poljana P. Miličevića 4

Contents